Life Experiences

Life Experiences

Steve Robertson

Rev. date: 10/31/2018

To order additional copies of this book, contact:
Xlibris
1-888-795-4274
www.Xlibris.com
Orders@Xlibris.com
786943

CONTENTS

Chapter 1: Hard Times

Right at this moment, in every part of the world, people are wondering what they can do to get ahead. Some are trying to develop a self-improvement plan to boost their self-esteem, while others are trying to take chances in the form of betting or gambling. But there is also that group that continues to wonder, dream, or just wish for some type of inheritance to come their way while living a somewhat-laidback life. One day, we may have a rude awakening, realizing we are in the same spot or situation as we were years ago. At this point, most of us may have given up on our ambition. I have learned that everybody wants something. It may be money, position, good health, prestige, a good marriage, or some special recognition.

When you feel like you do not have the opportunities someone else has, it is easy for you to get into the "blame game," meaning you cannot help what you were born into. You are just a victim of society at a given point in time. Sometimes you wonder if life is always fair. For example, picture a single mother trying to take care of her child who's born with some type of birth defect. No father, husband, or anyone else is there to help her. The mother cannot afford to provide the proper care for her child's needs. Even the hospitals and doctor's offices shun her because she didn't make enough money or have a certain income to provide for her child. Then the mother winds up shoplifting and selling items to come up with the financial means to take care of her child. Later on, the mother gets caught stealing and then goes to jail while her child is put in some type of medical ward. Who's footing the bill now?

Sometimes we think we have it bad. As I was growing up, I received a lot of positive and negative attention. It wasn't easy growing up in the projects. Every time you leave the community, someone tries to watch your every move. I'm not talking about parents or family members. I'm talking about the police or some kind of government organization. Every time a store gets robbed in a different community, the police comes to our neighborhood and rarely looks anywhere else. If something bad happens, they will come here first.

Once I witnessed a middle-aged man coming out of a grocery store, and he kept clutching at his chest. Just as soon as the man walked around the corner, he collapsed. I looked around to see if anybody else saw it, but there was no one around at that time. I didn't want to get involved because of all the hassle I received growing up by the police. I knew how to perform CPR, but I was very hesitant to do so. The man was dying right in front of me and needed medical attention. He gasped for air, and then he fell to the ground. He hit the pavement hard and couldn't breathe; his face was changing color quickly. So I began to perform CPR. I ripped his shirt open and took his pulse. Suddenly, I heard police sirens from a distance. I began to panic, thinking the police would blame the situation on me. I truly wanted to save the man's life and tell the police what happened. Then thoughts of how the police officials had treated me and my friends in the past started to enter my mind. I kept telling myself, "No, I must do the right thing!" But I ran.

Looking back, if I had a chance to do it again, I would have given that man CPR instead of running from the cops for two good reasons: First, a person was in "dying need" of medical attention, and I could have provided that while someone phoned the ambulance service. A person's life is worth saving (or trying to at least). Second, I have been living with this guilt ever since. I could have told the cops what happened without worrying if they believed me or not. It's just when a person has been hassled so much by the police, it could make a person turn the other way despite the situation. The biggest take away from this is that no matter what you do in life, no matter what your occupation is, apply the golden rule and we all will be better off.

At this point in my life, I felt like I had to get away from my surroundings. So I went to Minneapolis, Minnesota; I knew a well-known legendary musician there. It was during the winter months, and it was very cold. Before I reached my destination, I stopped on the side of the road, just gazing at the scenery. I put my heavy winter coat on top of my already layers of clothes. It was a heavily wooded area with hills and slopes that look very mesmerizing. So I decided to take a quick hike to enjoy this winter solitude. It was cold, in fact colder than I realized, so I kept moving into the wilderness, looking at the many different sceneries that I was not used to seeing. I spotted a lake; it was a good distance away, and the top of it was frozen. I wanted to get close, but it was becoming colder and colder. Finally, I decided to go back to my car because I couldn't take it anymore. As soon as I turned around, it started to snow. The wind was strong as well. After all this happened, it made me realize something; I was lost! The tracks I made on the ground were quickly being covered by snow. I kept walking, hoping that I was going in the right direction. I couldn't tell anymore, so I started wishing that I would run into someone who knew the way out. I kept wandering in the strong wind and snow that I grew numb and tired. The more I walked, the more I was convinced that I was lost. Then I passed out!

I remember waking up in a field, looking around, and I had a terrible feeling that something was wrong. It was spring! I was wearing a T-shirt, shorts, and tennis shoes. I said, "What the heck is going on here?" Even today, I continue to struggle to regain my memories of what happened while I was hiking. I still ask myself what kind of clothes I had on when I left my house. I know I was wearing winter clothes because it was winter and I was going up north. Where did the shorts and T-shirt come from? There are still a lot of unanswered questions, and if I had to do it again, I wouldn't! Thus far, these two different life experiences are enough to stunt a person's growth!

Chapter 2: In Training

After all these different life experiences, once again I decided to do something different— martial arts. It's known as a way of fighting (depending on how you are taught) and consists of graceful moves, powerful blows, and awesome kicks. People love to see this contact sport for various reasons. Fighters and practitioners train hard all year round to achieve the ultimate skill levels within their means. High-ranking instructors and fighters keep their mind sharp and their bodies intact. Martial art benefits a person in many ways.

When competing in full-contact matches, fighters use more than just their physical skills. They also use their mind in a high-capacity way. Because often, outthinking your opponent can mean you do not have to work as hard or take so many blows. When two fighters are evenly matched in skills, usually, the one that outthinks his opponent will win. But some fighters want to do more than just win; they want to hurt their opponent just for mere bragging rights. It's up to the individual to use their skills wisely.

Most people who want to learn are interested in self-defense only. They do not care about the fighting part. They just want to be able to defend themselves and/or their friends and family members in a hostile situation. Someone could threaten you or a family member. You could be shopping at a mall, and a person could come up to you and threaten you or your spouse. There are all kinds of scenarios you could be in where it becomes beneficial to know. A physical assault could happen to anyone at any time.

Others want to learn martial arts because of the fitness benefits it offers. It keeps your body well tuned, and you feel more energetic than before. Even when a person works all day, you're not as tired at the end of the day.

Martial arts can also help a person to comprehend life's challenges. It helps in everyday living when obstacles get in the way. It's like a problem-solving enhancement. Whether you are learning in school or doing on-the-job training, it can improve your ability to understand better. Some parents have noticed that their children's grades are slightly higher when their children become involved in martial arts. They see their comprehension level go up, and they become more focused on the issues that are before them. But let me not fail to mention that it also depends on the instructor. It pays to have a good, well-rounded instructor, and choosing the right one is essential.

So you see, martial arts can benefit a person in different ways. It's not all about fighting; it's more than that.

Some of my life stories are martial arts related. For example, the parents of an eight-year-old-girl came to me, saying their little girl comes home hungry every day from school. They also noticed that she has become jittery and is distancing herself from the family. They went to her teachers and asked what was going on. The teachers had no idea but mentioned that her grades were getting worse. So the parents took her to the doctor to get checked, and the doctor found nothing wrong. This went on for more than two months, and they did not see anything out of the ordinary. When the parents came to me, I asked them to bring their daughter over and let me talk to her. They did. When I talked to her, she could not look at me and kept her head down. I talked to her for about one minute, and she didn't want to talk. I told her parents that I have seen enough and for them to call me when they get home. So they called, and they told me again what the teachers were saying. The teachers kept insisting that they didn't see anything wrong. So I suggested that something was happening outside. I told the parents to ask their daughter if she goes outside during recess, and she said yes. I immediately said, "Bingo! That's it!" Then I told the parents to let me work with their daughter for a couple of months and it would be a good idea if one of them would go through the same training as well. They agreed. The father volunteered. Since I was already training my brother, I got him involved as well. I started training everyone in self-defense. One month rolled by, and she started talking to me and looking me in the eye (which is a good sign). So at that point, I introduced them to sparring techniques. I paired up with the eight year old, showing her how to spar. When she hit me, I fell hard, saying, "What did you do to me?" She started laughing and was really enjoying it. This was the very first time I got her to smile. An important milestone! Keep in mind that all this time, I never mentioned her situation at school. Two weeks of sparring went by, and I talked to her one on one. I stated to her that she do not have to take that anymore She looked at me, smiled, and said "what?" I got serious with her and then told her again; "Do not take it anymore what's going on in school." She was surprised and had a blank look on her face. She was quiet, and I kept looking at her. She finally said, "Okay, I won't." Keep in mind that I never asked her what was going on.

So the next school day came; she went outside during recess, and two older boys came up, wanting her lunch money again. She looked the boys in the eyes and said, "I'm not going to let you have my money anymore!" The boys said, "We told you what we were going to do if you don't give it to us." She just stood there, and then one boy reached out to push her, and she evaded him by stepping to the side and knocked him down! The other boy saw that, and he started running. That was the end of that long-drawn-out dilemma; the boys did not threaten her anymore. She told me the whole story after it was over, and she asked me how I knew about it. You guys can imagine how good I felt that I was on the right track all along without asking her what was going on. That was better than any trophy that I had ever won. She found a four-leaf clover and gave it to me. Her grades got better, and her confidence came back. She was a happy child again.

Chapter 3: Virtues

I really had a humble beginning. During my early childhood days, I learned how to mow yards. I remember using push mowers that didn't have a motor. Later on, I graduated to a push mower with a motor. I couldn't reach the top handle; I had to use the middle bar that goes across the handle. Weed eaters weren't invented yet, so I had to use grass shears. That's a job by itself, but when weed eaters came out, I bought three or four of them!

At one point, growing up, my brother and I lived in a housing project, and I can honestly say that at one time or another, I mowed every yard over there. That was my starting point. I made one dollar a yard. A few years later, that one dollar turned into two dollars a yard. I thought that I was on top of the world when that happened.

But listen, that experience taught me a valuable lesson. As I got older, I didn't forget where I came from. I went back to that neighborhood and mowed those yards for free. I'm not talking about one time; I'm talking about all summer long. I can still remember their names: Mrs. Arlene, Mrs. Lottie Laster, Mrs. Bertha Jones, Mr. and Mrs. Frank William, Mrs. Vessie Lou Flakes, and of course my grandmother, Mae L. Johnson. I did not forget where I came from.

Chapter 4: Achievements

At this point in life, I feel very fortunate for having the chance to experience different walks of life because I'm beginning to see how it can benefit others as well. As life goes on and you have lived or are living a constructive life, that's value added to yourself. Why not share it with others? After all, that's what He wants us to do.

I remember when I was looking at young people's faces while we were growing up in the projects. Since we were all so innocent in the beginning, kids couldn't see poverty, hardships, and the struggle it takes to make it day by day. In their eyes, that's how it was supposed to be. Some will grow up and do it all over again generations after generations. It's like their world is on common ground, but there's nowhere to go if they hang around. Some really do not realize there's another world out there that they can invite themselves to.

I'm not discrediting the projects because they do serve their purpose. That's a good thing. But to those who are thinking that's how it is supposed to be, you have options. So just spread your wings and fly like an eagle soaring over the mountain tops and demanding the sky. You can do it—just try! Set reachable goals for yourself and give yourself time to achieve them. Don't be afraid to ask for help when you need it. Use the resources around you; seek and you shall find! You cannot eat the whole elephant at one time. Break it down into small bites.

When you have finally achieved your goals, let it lead to bearing good fruits with others as well.

Chapter 5: Hobbies

People, corporate America is great, but you cannot always depend on it. If you believe in yourself, invest in yourself!

I remember a lot of people looking for advice when they lost their job. I tried to help them. First thing I asked was, are there any type of skills or trade you're good at? Two individuals spoke up; the first one said he was good at being a mechanic, and the other individual said he was good at woodwork. I said, "Okay, that's great. You both have good skill sets." Then I told them that they can turn their hobbies into a source of income until they find another steady job. They both replied that they did not have the tools to work with. People, this is what I mean: "If you believe in yourself, invest in yourself." Now here are two individuals out of work, but they can support their families if only they had the right tools. It is easier to buy the tools while you're working than it is when you're not. If you believe in yourself, invest in yourself.

Chapter 6: Character

Now let's look at one more type of scenario: sometimes bad luck hits us in different ways. An able man who was down on his luck goes to a family member, asking for some food to eat because he was hungry. So the family member gives him fish. There's nothing wrong with that, especially when someone is down on luck. But what would be better? Instead of giving him fish, give him a pole and take him fishing. Now you have given this man two things: the tools to catch his own and a step closer to becoming independent again because sometimes it becomes a mind-set.

The morale of my story is that sometimes we can help ourselves. If we start taking ownership of our lives instead of doing the blame game, we can get a lot more done. Let's not stand for nothing and fall for anything. Failing to prepare is like preparing to fail. Between all of us, we need to build more bridges and fewer fences. Instead of tearing somebody down, build somebody up!

Be constructive. Sometimes doing something worthwhile can pay off twofold. This is my opinion: If you want to be a janitor in life, don't just be an ordinary janitor. Be a great one. Show some passion. Success is measured not so much by the position that one has reached in life but by the obstacles one has overcome trying to succeed. In other words, if you fall, pick yourself up and play ball. Don't have a pity party because you fell. It happens to us all. If you reach for the moon and can't grab it, take some of the stars along the way so you won't come back empty-handed. That itself would be knowledge you can use. Build on it. Take that ball again and run with it.

This is especially for the young people. Instead of surrounding yourself with all the wrong faces and spending your time in all the wrong places and putting faith in things that tear you down, go out and find something positive to do. Develop a trade or gain some experience and it will take you to a point where there will be less confusion, which also eliminates a lot of fear, less boredom and less shame.

At first, I was the child, the son, and the father, and now I'm the man with a better soul. I'm at that road. While I'm here, I can walk it with someone or walk it alone just as long as I stay on the same path with the Lord.

Growing should be a never-ending process. We grow in different ways. We can all see and understand the physical aspect of growing, even getting to a certain point where we all virtually stop in that perspective. But what about growing our knowledge through reading and searching for ideas and answers to keep developing our mind, increasing our knowledge, and improving our motor skills? What better way can we spend our time than in pursuit of learning and defining our spirituality. This will take a lifetime.

Joseph Gorman is the man who comes to my mind with this type of request. He really enjoys this never-ending adventure. We can discuss a certain chapter or verse and get a clearer meaning from it. So what does this tell me? This tells me that it was already there. Some of us are ever so growing in ways that are unimaginable. So it pays for us to go back and revisit something that we have already read but did not get a full understanding of. Sometimes when we walk away from it or put additional time between it, the message becomes clearer.

This is how I take it: The message hasn't changed since it's been written. Also, the same message could give us something different depending where we are in life and what we need. But the message is concrete and solid. You can read a certain verse now and leave it alone. Go back and read it ten years later and see if it has a more profound meaning to you. If so, you could be at a different stage in your life and get a deeper meaning out of it. Even though it has the same words, somehow you get something different out of it. Yet the words are unchanging!

Joseph Gorman has a unique way of putting things in perspective. For someone who can do this, it is a talent within itself.

Chapter 8: Appreciation

This journey is very special to me, and I am proud to have this opportunity of sharing these experiences with you. I hope it will inspire you along the way at some point in your life. We all need some kind of inspiration while we are here trying to make it. It took me over thirty years to write this. It's also very sentimental to me. My heart and soul are poured into this journey, and it will not be completed unless I talk about my pastor.

My pastor, Mr. Billy Williams, means a lot to me. I really mean this. I care so much about him and really enjoy every conversation we share together. We can sit down and talk for hours and reminisce over the hard, challenging times we had growing up. You may say we can all do that with someone we grew up with, but there's a little difference; we are a generation apart.

When I talk with the pastor one on one, it's a spiritual upliftment for me. And somewhere in our conversation, some similarities we have come up. Whether they are in the present or past, some similarities always reveal themselves. But they are always uplifting. For example, I had driven a pair of mules pulling a wagon. Even more so, after a day of picking cotton, we used to load the wagon with the cotton we picked, and I would drive many miles to a cotton gin. That was the best time of my life. I thought that I was on top of the world. Then the pastor told me of his similar experiences driving a team of mules. But he just could not picture me doing this, especially because of my age. That conversation lasted for hours, and it was very uplifting to us both. Then we started talking about how we used to make molasses from sugarcanes. We would hitch up a mule to a mill grinder, and the mule would walk in circles around this grinder while we steadily pushed sorghum canes into the mill grinder and started seeing the molasses flowing out of it. Oh yeah, those were the days!

Sometimes I would daydream and hope that maybe one Christmas, instead of getting a car, I may be lucky enough to get a nice team of mules. I mean, it just doesn't get any better than that!

I can also remember the very first time when my father, Jessie, and his brother, Uncle Willie, asked me to help cook for our annual family reunion on the Fourth of July. That was like my heaven on earth! Excited was too small of a word to use to describe what that meant to me. I could not believe that I made the "ranks" to be considered as one of the main cooks. That was one of my biggest dreams that came true. At times, the reunion was attended by over one to three hundred family members and friends. It's always amazing to watch my two aunties, Darlene and Ann, making their famous stew in those big black kettles using only natural ingredients. Amazing! The taste is simply unmatched!

I can remember another special occasion that my uncle Willie and I cooked a whole hog together for a church's 150th anniversary. The local TV broadcast station was there reporting this event. My uncle looked at me and said, "Steve, we cook together like Arm and Hammer!" That was an honor coming from him.

So, Pastor, I really enjoyed the conversations we had together. I'm speaking for myself, but I bet others would agree as well that it's so good being around someone that believes in you. That itself is an inspiration to just keep doing good things for others. Now what can I say that hasn't been told? Pastor, you bring out the best in us! Thank you!

Chapter 9: A King

Let me share this with you. I just want to give you all something to think about. Let's stop and take a minute on how we see things for the first time. Everybody has heard of first impressions, right? We tend to draw conclusions when we first meet someone. Then we start to form our own opinion even though during this time, we do not have enough to go on. Yet that does not stop us. Think about it. Our mind or our brain takes a snapshot of that moment. That's all! Because our first opinion is coming from our head and not our heart. This reminds me of an old story that's out there somewhere.

There's a story about this king who lived a long time ago. He was the ruler of all the land that was before him. At times, he would get bored because he had conquered everything around him. He started to look for something different to do. He always wanted to hunt but didn't know how because he was always protected. So the king decided to go hunting, but he would only take one servant that he trusted more than anyone else in this world. He went to this servant and told him to drop everything because they would go hunting. The servant dropped everything he was doing, and they both headed toward the woods. The servant spotted a wild board and pointed at it and told his king to shoot it. So the king aimed and pulled the hammer back and squeezed the trigger. But nothing happened. No gun shot noise, no anything! Suddenly, the king began to feel severe thumb pain. His thumb was in the way when he pulled the trigger, and it was smashed really bad. The servant saw what happened and took the king to their local healer (which is a doctor now). The healer said, "This thumb is really bad!" He told the king that his thumb had to be removed. The king was in so much pain, so he told the healer to just do it. So the healer sawed his thumb off, and the servant looked at it and said, "All is good." The king got so mad at him and asked, "What did you say?" The servant repeated himself and calmly said, "All is good!" The king was really mad at this point and told his guards to lock him up. "Keep him behind bars for a full year!" No one has ever seen the king this mad before.

Then three months had passed, and the king's hand was already free of pain. So he decided to go hunting again, but this time by himself. When he started walking through the woods, he began to have a funny feeling;

maybe it was because he was all alone and wasn't used to that. Before he could realize it, he was surrounded by a rival tribe from far away. They were cannibals, so they started to tie him to a pole and cook him alive. As they were tying him to the pole, one of the tribe members noticed that he had a thumb missing. So all the tribe members got together and came to the conclusion to let him go because they wanted a whole body with no missing parts. As soon as they let the king go, he ran back to where he locked his servant up and told him that he was right. All is good! Then he began to tell his servant what had happened and how he was captured by the rival tribe, but they let him go because his thumb was missing. The king was so happy that his life was spared. So he told the servant that he was going to let him go and that he was sorry for locking him up all this time. The king also told the servant that he was right all along that "all is good." The servant looked at the king and smiled.

Just before the king let the servant go, he asked him if he was mad at him for locking him up. The servant smiled and said, "All is good!" The king looked at him and said, "What's wrong with you? I locked you up all this time, and you are not mad?" The servant said no. The king asked why. The servant said, "If you did not lock me up, I would have been with you." The king said, "Yes, and so what? What's wrong with that?" The servant said, "I have both of my thumbs!"

So what is it I'm trying to say?

Chapter 10: Rediscovering Yourself

Sometimes life feels really good when certain situations are going your way. You put life on "cruise control" and just enjoy what you have built for yourself. Or maybe you and your family or spouse are absorbing all the good things that life has thrown your way. Life is great.

Then something unexpected comes and rocks your world. You're losing your financial grip at home, or your job's business has taken a turn for the worst. Your spouse is not happy, or the relationship isn't what it once was. You look in the mirror, or you see your picture on the wall with one eye starring at nothing and the other one trying to focus through all the tears. So I'm here to say: let's rediscover ourselves and our own life!

This is what I mean about rediscovering ourselves. Sometimes it pays to go back in time to reevaluate yourself. I'm not talking about physically going back in time. Just sit back, relax, and reminisce; just reminisce. Look at some of the fruits you came from. I can still remember just like it was yesterday when my grandmother gathered up some kids in the neighborhood to encourage them to go to youth revival. Sometimes the kids did go, and for those who went, she gave them a penny each to put in the collection plate.

I can even remember when my mother, Edna, moved up in her nursing profession. She was the first registered nurse to be promoted as a head nurse and beyond in this area.

What I'm trying to say is, whenever things are not going your way, just stop and take note. You see, nearly everyone feels insignificant at one point or another. Nevertheless, you may be great on the football field, or you may be an excellent basketball player. You may even be a great cook. But on the other hand, you may be terrible in a chemistry lab or not so good at sewing. You may have a 50/50 fan base, meaning you're good with this crowd, but you're totally ignored by another crowd.

Let's face it. There are things that you can do, but I will struggle with! On the other hand, there are things that I can do that you will struggle with!

What I'm trying to say is that we all have different specialties, each and every one of us. Sometimes it pays for us to figure out what we are really good at. And if you're not making a living out of it, maybe it can become a hobby or even a small business, which could be a second source of income. There are all kind of ways we can rediscover ourselves. Now that's one end of the spectrum; let's change the scenario and look at this in a different perspective.

You know it's easy for some of us to feel down and out when people put us down. It's hard to stand up and be counted when you feel alone and the crowd is against you. Some people even tend to kick others, especially when they are down. So at this point, where can you discover your true value?

We all are made in God's image and created to do great things! Life may chip away at our souls, but God sent His only Son into our world to take away our pain and sins while offering us a new start.

Jesus Christ sees you as an incredibly valuable person. He sees past your hurt and your pain. He recognizes that you have real worth. Better yet, He is ready to take away the mess you have created in your life! When we receive God's gift of forgiveness, we discover that we are chosen, handpicked by God for a relationship with Jesus Christ that will never end!

You have to remember that Jesus was perfect in every way. But some were not happy with Him. While Jesus taught us to love God and each other, evil men were plotting against Him. So when they captured

Him, He was tried unfairly. They sentenced Him to die on the cross.

Jesus died for our sake. He paid the price for our wrongdoing. Because He died in our place, we found God's forgiveness.

But the story didn't end there. Three days later, He rose!

Now the Lord is willing to forgive us for all our sins. He knows us better than we do. He knows our weakness, yet He offers to make a way for us. But only if we ask Him and do the things that He wants us to do.

So next time when you feel down and out with nowhere to go, when you have issues you don't know how to deal with, and when you have no one to talk to, look here!

Our Father who art in heaven, hallowed be Thy name. Thy kingdom come. Thy will be done on earth as it is in heaven. Give us this day our daily bread, and forgive us our trespasses, as we forgive those who trespasses against us, and lead us not into temptation, but deliver us from evil. For Thine is the kingdom, and the power, and the glory, for ever and ever. Amen.

Now when you look in the mirror or see your picture on the wall with one eye staring at nothing and the other one focused, these are much different tears!

Chapter 11: Congregation

I just want to share a personal moment with you. A few years back when I left a certain church, I had my reasons, and I didn't share them with anyone. I felt a change coming. Something was urging me to grow. At first, I ignored it. But it got stronger. It didn't go away. The Lord revealed himself to me and said, "Enough!" I have been "spinning my wheels" long enough. He reminded me; this is not who you are.

So the first thing that hit my mind was to leave this church. I just felt like I couldn't grow there. It was just one abstract thing that I felt would get in the way.

For instance, some people try to judge and prejudge you, even though we should not judge others the way we do. I understand that; this happens virtually everywhere you go; I get that. Even at times when you speak during Sunday school or any type of group discussions, others try to find faults in what you are saying, especially when it doesn't involve them at all. Looking for some kind of injustice in what you have said. They will get upset and try to get others to join in as well. Jesus said it best when Peter asked him, "Which is he that betrays you?" Jesus told him in a roundabout way, "What business is it of yours?" (John 21:20–23).

Keep this in mind; there's good and bad in all of us; if a person tries to "judge" you; watch what side they choose to judge because really, they are showing you want kind of person they are! (Matthew 7:1-2)

Please keep this in mind; I'm not speaking of all churches or all members, just some that

I personally encountered. Once more; this doesn't implies to all members as well. I have met; talked and discussed bible scriptures with several members whereas we all enjoyed sharing our different views and respecting one another's insight. Being God's children; he gives of different spiritual gifts that are meant to be shared with one another.

This shows unity among us and reflects God's design for how things are to become. There are many good Christians within the body of the churches which makes learning and being there so much enjoyable. They are so good to be around giving you great encouragement of keep going in the spiritual way. Sometimes I often wonder what the real Christians think when they see the "so-calls" behave in this negative manner. It could be just as distasteful for them as well. But the real Christians still display their meek like appearances. Those are the ones that are admirable.

Picture this; A person "comes out of the street" getting his/her life together by trying to drop their bad habits and iniquities; replacing them with rightful things and what God wants us to do. Even participating in church and Sunday school as well. But during this time the first 1 or 2 years this person sometimes has "setbacks" but never gives up. Right at this moment is when this person realizes that you cannot serve two "Gods" (there's only one real one). So he finds a way deep down inside of him to "feed" the one he wants to serve while starving the one he wants to get rid of. Another two years past and now this person has "dropped" their bad habits and the iniquities. But the "so-call" Christians are virtually at the same place (behavior) during all of this time.

So I ask you; who have made the biggest improvements in their life?

The "So Calls" are mirrors, vanities and illusions. Seeing others but not themselves. If you have been listening closely to what I am saying is: Struggling is not only happening in the streets, it's also happening in some churches to.

For those who are looking for a church, it's more meaningful and joyful when everyone realizes that we are in this together. The moral of this story is; do not let people deter you; go and get your spirituality on. Do what's pleasing to God; let man say what he wants.

I'm going on this great mission to do what the Lord said to do. Sometimes it's hard to worship with the ones who frown upon you, yet they do some of the same things (Romans 2:1).

So for those who are turning their life around for the better, let no man deter you for they do not have a Heaven or Hell to put you in. They are going to be judged just like you, but the biggest difference is: it's from the one who truly qualifies.

There are a lot of churches that I really enjoyed fellowshipping with. The pastors of three different churches asked me to teach Sunday school when the regular teacher was absent. I taught Sunday school in three different churches in the surrounding counties. I also got chances to cook for the members and led the church in prayers. Deacons and pastors called me weekly to discuss scriptures. I even participated in church history programs. It was an honor, and I was so grateful to be a part of it.

Attending Sunday school and church is rewarding and delightful. I did find what I was looking for when I was out there searching. I *turned* during the times I was attending other churches. The feeling was unmatched by anything else; if it takes getting away sometimes to achieve what you are looking for; go for it for no man can decide your faith. When this change started to work on me, I was slowly letting some of my iniquities go. I made confessions at church; I was denying them in the beginning but was finally getting rid of them. It was a process. Of course, as people, we all sin; I'm talking about the "uncontrollable desires." So God's words were with me like never before. During this time when I was studying the Bible, God's words became clearer to me. Like a vision, I could see them and what they meant. What I was trying to explain before is that God's words do not change; we change. For us to enter God's kingdom, we must be born again; being born again will bring changes.

We can read His words today and leave them alone for five years. Go back and reread the same verse and we may find a more profound meaning of the same words we read before. Sometimes we have to get to something or go through something to see something differently. God wants unity among us, and He wants us to share our spiritual gifts. Our spiritual gifts are not the same, so He wants us to share. If you get a different meaning out of something that God reveals to you than someone else, it's doesn't necessarily means that one of you are wrong. You're probably in two different places or stages in your lives. God gives us what we need, and our needs may not be the same. If God gives the same spiritual gifts, what are we going to share? He knows we are not going to see all His words the same, and that's when we should come together; let's share.

At times when I read the Bible, I will read more than one version. I sometimes read the King James Version, and at other times, I read the New International Version as well. At times, I find it very rewarding looking at more than one aspect of a given subject. Church is so much better when we all build bridges instead of fences

Have you ever stopped and wonder why when someone is doing better in life it brings out hatred in some others? Instead of bringing hatred out- letting it show- why not step aside to make a way for those who wants to go?

(Psalms 35)

Chapter 12: The Price of Disobedience

Along my journey while visiting other churches, I witnessed two young boys come into a church to hear Sunday school and church services. They kept coming Sunday after Sunday, never saying a word but listening and absorbing everything that what said. One Sunday, the preacher finally made his way to the two boys, and the boys let the preacher know that they would like to join the services and one day get baptized and be church members. The preacher told them, "Okay, that is great! We will be glad to have you!" The two boys were so happy that they kept coming Sunday after Sunday, but the preacher never acknowledged them again in any kind of regard. So finally, the two boys asked the preacher again when they could join and be baptized to be a part of the church. The preacher's answer was next Sunday. You know what? That next Sunday never came. The boys were hurt, and they just stopped coming.

Like I said earlier, some of us can't see the forest because of the trees. Those boys turned to the church for help; they could have been lost souls just begging for help to be saved. They came to the right place, which was the church. What are the two boys going to do now?

I have to admit. It seems like my life story is in the Bible too. You remember when Moses led his people out from Egypt? They weren't the only ones wandering around in the wilderness for forty years. It seems like that's what I have also done for the last forty years until a few years ago when God was getting my attention. That feeling was so deep, it seeped into my bones. When the Lord was getting my attention, it reminded me of a song by a group called the Gap Band. The Gap Band was a group from the eighties, and I remembered the last song on a particular album was called "Running In and Out of My Life." That's what the Lord was telling me. Steve, you can't keep running in and out of my life!

Right then, I took to the Bible; I looked through it, looking for a Bible story to learn. My eyes stopped on the three Hebrew boys. When I read that story, something was telling me to learn it, know it, and speak it. Guess what? I did.

I told the whole story to a church audience without looking or reading one word. To me, that was my moment of freedom, just like the people of Israel coming out of Egypt.

Break the chains! Break the chains! I see the light!

Okay, moving on. Now can I talk about my favorite book in the world?

Let's turn to Psalm 103:20.

Bless the Lord, ye his angels, that excel in strength, that do his commandments, hearkening unto the voice of his word.

What's key about this verse is that the Bible says that there's a reward when we obey. God makes us strong, and He increases our strength.

So this got me thinking, if God increases our strength when we obey, what happens when we disobey? Good question. When we disobey, God takes away some of our strength. Let's go to the Bible to see what it has to say. Let's start from the beginning with Adam and Eve.

In the beginning, Adam was strong. He had dominion of the whole world. There was nothing on earth above him. The woman (Eve) was on his side, and she was also strong and had a high position on earth.

At this time, the serpent was strong as well, standing around and going to and from.

So when they disobeyed God, he took away some of their strength.

The snake that was once walking is now on the ground, crawling everywhere he wants to go.

The woman lost her power of position. Before, she was beside the man. Now, God moved her behind the man (biblically speaking). She also knew no pain before she sinned. Now when she bears a child, she will become weak and feel pain during labor.

And to the man who had authority over all earthly things, the Lord said, "You shall eat bread in the sweat of your face until you return to the ground in which you came from!" So look at this, He made them weak.

You see, at that time, nothing on earth was over Adam. Now the Lord put death over Adam. The Bible tells that no man has the power to deliver himself in the day of death. You see, death was under Adam in the beginning, but now God put death over him. Death is strong, and it's been reigning ever since!

All I'm saying is, when we keep disobeying God, He takes away something from us; He makes us weaker. You don't have to take my word for it; just look at what happened to Samson. God made him weaker when he told a secret that he should not have told.

Look at the house of David. David and his sons committed a lot of sins, even to each other. They committed adultery, and his sons had relationships with concubines and even their half-sister. One of his sons also went in and killed them. So God weakened the house of David because of disobedience.

Let us not forget about Jezebel. Jezebel was evil and conniving. She would turn people against people. She was the kind who would throw a rock at you and then hide her hands! She married King Ahab, and one day, he came home like he was heartbroken. Jezebel asked him what was wrong. He said that Naboth would not sell him the vineyard he wanted. Jezebel asked him, "Ain't you the king?" She told him in so many words, "Don't worry about it! I'll get it for you." Later in the story, she was thrown to the dogs!

If we know these things from the past, why are we still doing them? This is what I'm working on right now, getting rid of iniquities as humanly possible. I just walked through the Bible and showed how God made us weaker when we disobeyed.

Now, on the other hand, I found the opposite to be true if we obey his words. Do you remember in Psalms chapter 103:verse20 that his angel that does his commandments excels in strength?

The good book tells me that Caleb was eighty-five years old, still as strong today (being eighty-five) as he was the day Moses led them out of Egypt. Caleb must have had a well of water that he could draw from.

Now there are basically two types of well water. Let's look at John 4:13: "Jesus answered and said unto her, Whosoever drinketh of this water shall thirst again."

That verse reminds me of the times I spent with my grandmother. I remember one time she told the menfolk that the well was dry. And we all know how essential water is to us. Not only do we use water on the inside, but also we use it on the outside. Things are not just right when you are out of water. So all the menfolk gathered to go and find some water. They went to the well and dug deeper. They didn't stop until they got wet. So this made me stop and think: what good is a well if it runs dry?

A dry well can't help nobody! We can relate this to John 4:13: "Whosoever drinketh of this water shall thirst again."

Now remember that I said earlier that there are basically two types of well. This well of my grandmother's is one type. For the other type of well, let's go to the good book and find out. Look at John chapter 4 verse:14: "But whosoever drinketh of the water that I shall give him shall never thirst; but the water that I shall give him shall be in him a well of water springing up into everlasting life."

This means, for all God's children, he puts this type of well in us for safekeeping, and we can continually draw on it without fearing of this well ever going dry.

Let me go to the Bible and show you what I'm talking about.

What happened when King Nebuchadnezzar threw Shadrach, Meshach, and Abednego into the fiery furnace? Before they could call on the Lord, he was already there! Nebuchadnezzar had to take a closer look. He asked his men, "Did we not throw three men into the fire?" The men replied yes. The king said, "Yet I see four walking around in the fire with no kind of hurt!"

What about Jonah? He was thrown overboard into a fearsome, raging sea. As he was thrown into the sea, a large fish swallowed him up and steadily went deeper into the sea, For three days and three nights, Jonah was in the belly of that fish. Needless to say, Jonah began to worry. He went deep into the well that's inside of him, crying out for the Lord, knowing he's in trouble and needing some help.

The Lord didn't say a word to Jonah, but He spoke to the fish! The fish came up from the deep water and delivered him on dry land. So the next time you call on the Lord, He may not speak directly to you, but the problem you're facing, he already spoken to! So remember, if you want to be strong, you must first obey God.

Thank you!

The Stages Of Life!

Growth can be a beautiful thing when you
keep everything in the right perspective.

Life has a way of adding value to your worth.
In the beginning when you were just barely
old enough to get out and experience life-
you may felt like donating yourself to science
fiction. But to the near ending of your personal
journeys which consist of ups and downs like
a jet plane running in and out of bad weather-
feeling all the turbulences that it caused.
You're trying to hold it steady while waiting
on better days and if you finally make it
through; you can come out feeling priceless!

Negativity: sometimes in order
to go forward we have to:

Throw it all up against the wall, to
the wall with it all; then move on

This journey is heading toward
the number 7-Complete

My mind was first into rock and roll,
then jazz, then rhythm and blues and
now this spiritual thing called soul!

Another Sirexcellent Productions
sirexcellent@charter.net

Another Sirexcellent Productions

This book is dedicated to my dear mother, Edna

To my son, Christopher

To my brother, Tony

To my father, Jessie

To my cousin Wayne

To my grandmothers,

Mae L. Johnson

Ruth Robertson

Special thanks and dedications
to my grandfather,

Mr. Detroit Robertson

sirexcellent@charter.net

CPSIA information can be obtained
at www.ICGtesting.com
Printed in the USA
BVHW031152220122
626773BV00005B/480